CRIME Solvers

Serial Killer FILE

The Doctor of Death Investigation

by Mikaela Sitford

Consultant: Dr. John P. Cassella
Principal Lecturer in Forensic Science
Staffordshire University, England

BEARPORT PUBLISHING

New York, New York

Credits

Cover, © 2006 James Steidl/James Group Studios inc./istockphoto.com, © Hans Neleman/ Stone/Getty Images, and © Cavendish Press; Title Page, © Cavendish Press; 4, © Cavendish Press; 5T, © Manchester Evening News/M.E.N Syndication; 5B, © Manchester Evening News/ M.E.N Syndication; 6, © Cavendish Press; 7T, © Cavendish Press; 7B, © Mauro Fermariello/ Science Photo Library; 8, © Shutterstock; 9T, © Cavendish Press; 9B, © Cavendish Press; 10T, © Cavendish Press; 10B, © Cavendish Press; 11T, © Colin Cuthbert/Science Photo Library; 11B, © Cavendish Press; 12T, © Cavendish Press; 12B, © Dr. Jurgen Scriba/Science Photo Library; 13, © Cavendish Press; 14, © Manchester Evening News/M.E.N Syndication; 15T, © Cavendish Press; 15B, © Cavendish Press; 16, © PA/PA Archive/PA Photos; 17T, © Cavendish Press; 17B, © Timothy Large/istockphoto; 18, © Phil Noble/PA Archive/PA Photos; 19T, © Shutterstock; 19B, © Cavendish Press; 20, © Cavendish Press; 21L, © Shutterstock; 21R, © PA/PA Archive/PA Photos; 22, © Manchester Evening News/M.E.N Syndication; 23T, © PA/PA Archive/PA Photos; 23B, © Shutterstock; 24, © Manchester Evening News/M.E.N Syndication; 25L, © Cavendish Press; 25R, © Cavendish Press; 28, © Manchester Evening News/M.E.N Syndication; 29, © Mauro Fermariello/Science Photo Library; 30, © Shutterstock.

Every effort has been made by ticktock Entertainment Ltd. to trace copyright holders. We apologize in advance for any omissions. We would be pleased to insert the appropriate acknowledgments in any subsequent edition of this publication.

Publisher: Kenn Goin
Editorial Director: Adam Siegel
Project Editor: Dinah Dunn
Creative Director: Spencer Brinker
Original Design: ticktock Entertainment Ltd.

Library of Congress Cataloging-in-Publication Data

Sitford, Mikaela.
Serial killer file : the doctor of death investigation / by Mikaela Sitford.
p. cm. — (Crime solvers)
Includes bibliographical references and index.
ISBN-13: 978-1-59716-551-8 (library binding)
ISBN-10: 1-59716-551-4 (library binding)
1. Shipman, Harold Frederick, 1946– 2. Homicide—England—Manchester—Case studies—Juvenile literature. 3. Physicians—Malpractice—England—Manchester—Juvenile literature. 4. Serial murderers—England—Manchester—Biography—Juvenile literature. 5. Serial murder investigation—England—Manchester—Case studies—Juvenile literature. I. Title.

RA1123.S57 2008
364.152'3092—dc22

2007017957

2 Orchard Business Centre, North Farm Road, Tunbridge Wells, Kent, TN2 3XF, UK

Published in the United States of America by Bearport Publishing Company, Inc.

For more information, write to Bearport Publishing Company, Inc., 101 Fifth Avenue, Suite 6R, New York, New York 10003. Printed in the United States of America.

10 9 8 7 6 5 4 3 2 1

Contents

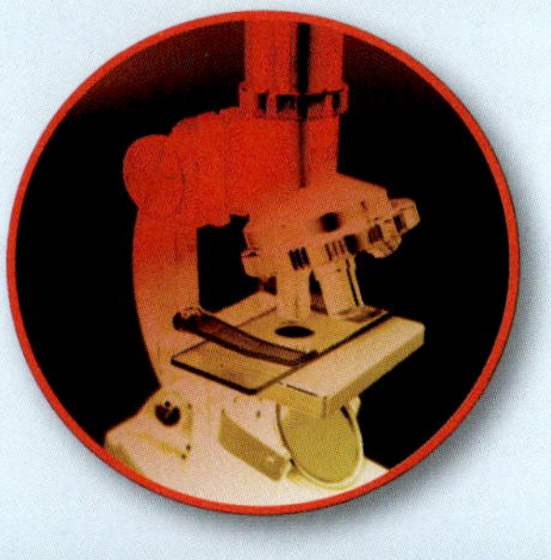

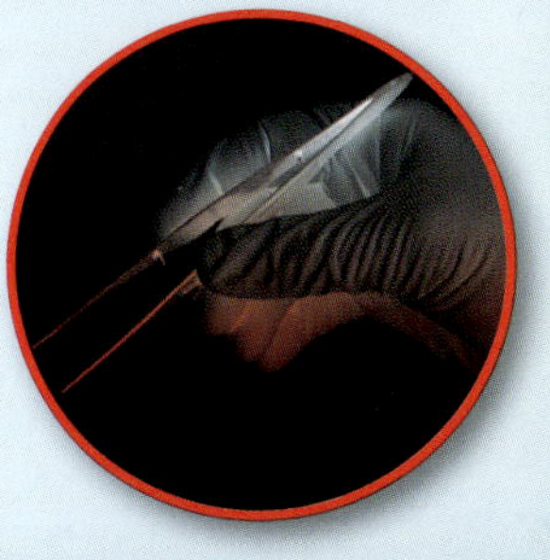

The Death of Kathleen Grundy

On June 24, 1998, Kathleen Grundy was supposed to meet some friends for lunch. When she didn't show up, her friends began to worry. They went to her house to see if she was all right.

They knocked on Kathleen Grundy's door, but there was no response. When they pushed open the unlocked door, her friends found her lying on a sofa. She was curled up as if asleep. Kathleen Grundy wasn't asleep, however. She was dead!

Mrs. Grundy's doctor, Harold Shipman, was called and came right over. He did not seem shocked by her death. He wrote that she died of "old age" on her **death certificate**. This surprised people who knew her. One friend described Kathleen Grundy as "a 25-year-old in an 80-year-old body."

Mrs. Grundy's home, Loughrigg Cottage

Kathleen's daughter, Angela Woodruff, spoke with Dr. Shipman. She learned that he had visited her mother that morning. Angela asked what caused her mother's death. He said that she had been sick and probably suffered a heart attack. This didn't make any sense to Angela. She was close with her mother. She would have known if she was ill. Soon, Angela would receive even more puzzling news.

Dr. Harold Shipman

FACT FILE

A Mysterious Death

The victim:
Kathleen Grundy, an 81-year-old woman who had once been the mayor of Hyde, England

Date of death:
June 24, 1998

Crime scene:
Kathleen Grundy's home, Loughrigg Cottage, where she lived alone

Kathleen Grundy

A Suspicious Will

Angela Woodruff was a lawyer. She handled all of her mother's legal work, including her **will**.

A few weeks after her mother's death, Angela was surprised to receive a new will from a law office in Hyde. They had received it the day Mrs. Grundy died. Badly written and typed, the new will left nothing to Angela. Everything Mrs. Grundy owned was to go to Dr. Harold Shipman.

Mrs. Grundy's affection for the doctor was well known. She was one of his many devoted patients. He took care of more than 3,000 people in Hyde. Many of them were old women. However, it seemed unlikely that Mrs. Grundy would leave everything to Dr. Shipman without telling her daughter.

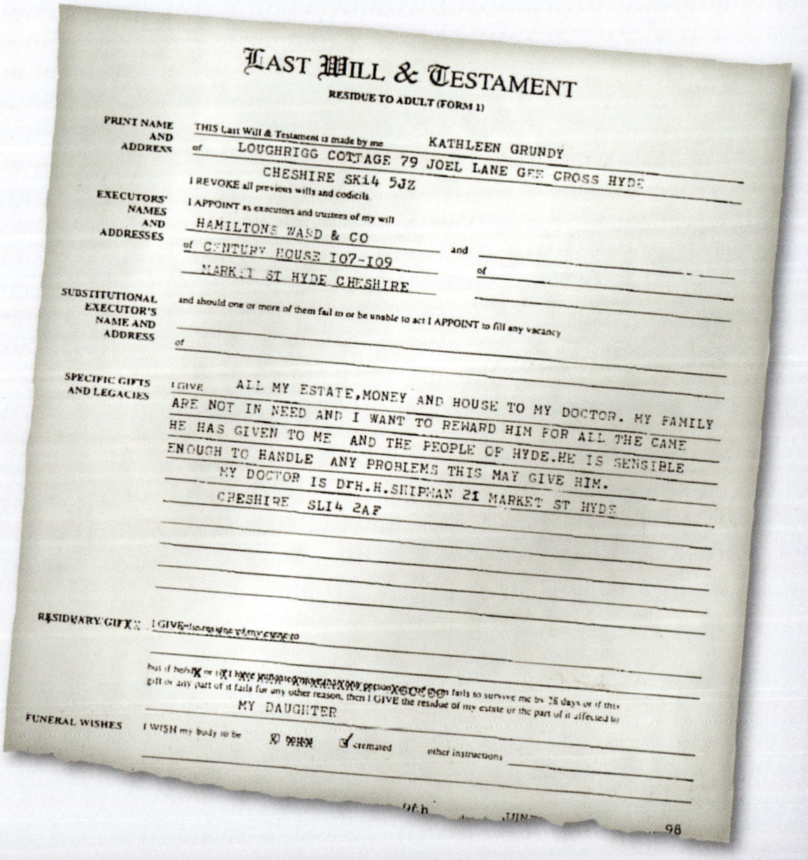
LAST WILL & TESTAMENT
RESIDUE TO ADULT (FORM 1)

PRINT NAME AND ADDRESS
THIS Last Will & Testament is made by me KATHLEEN GRUNDY
of LOUGHRIGG COTTAGE 79 JOEL LANE GEE CROSS HYDE
CHESHIRE SK14 5JZ
I REVOKE all previous wills and codicils

EXECUTORS' NAMES AND ADDRESSES
I APPOINT as executors and trustees of my will
HAMILTONS WARD & CO and
of CENTURY HOUSE 107-109 of
MARKET ST HYDE CHESHIRE

SUBSTITUTIONAL EXECUTOR'S NAME AND ADDRESS
and should one or more of them fail to or be unable to act I APPOINT to fill any vacancy
of

SPECIFIC GIFTS AND LEGACIES
I GIVE ALL MY ESTATE,MONEY AND HOUSE TO MY DOCTOR. MY FAMILY
ARE NOT IN NEED AND I WANT TO REWARD HIM FOR ALL THE CARE
HE HAS GIVEN TO ME AND THE PEOPLE OF HYDE.HE IS SENSIBLE
ENOUGH TO HANDLE ANY PROBLEMS THIS MAY GIVE HIM.
MY DOCTOR IS DrH.H.SHIPMAN 21 MARKET ST HYDE
CHESHIRE SL14 2AF

RESIDUARY GIFT I GIVE the residue of my estate to

but if he/she or if I have [illegible] fails to survive me by 28 days or if this gift or any part of it fails for any other reason, then I GIVE the residue of my estate or the part of it affected to
MY DAUGHTER

FUNERAL WISHES I WISH my body to be ☒ [illegible] ☑ cremated other instructions

98

Mrs. Grundy's new will was the first clue in a major investigation.

Angela began to **investigate**. She spoke with the two **witnesses** who had signed the new will. Both said Dr. Shipman had asked them to sign a piece of paper, but not a will. Angela figured out that Dr. Shipman had copied their signatures onto the will.

Angela began to wonder if Dr. Shipman had murdered her mother to get her money. She decided to go to the police.

Angela Woodruff was surprised her mother died so suddenly.

FACT FILE

The Fingerprint Evidence

- When a person touches a surface, his or her fingers leave marks called fingerprints. No two people have the same ones.
- The police examined Kathleen Grundy's will for fingerprints. None belonged to her. However, they did find one at the bottom of a page—it belonged to Dr. Shipman.

Police keep a record of all known criminals' fingerprints in a computer file.

Linda Reynolds's Warning

The death of Kathleen Grundy was not the first time someone had concerns about Dr. Shipman. In March 1998, Dr. Linda Reynolds had gone to the police. She was worried that a large number of Dr. Shipman's patients were dying **suspiciously** and then being **cremated**.

In fact, Dr. Shipman's patients died five times more often than the patients of other doctors in the area. Dr. Reynolds thought Shipman might be killing his patients with some sort of drug.

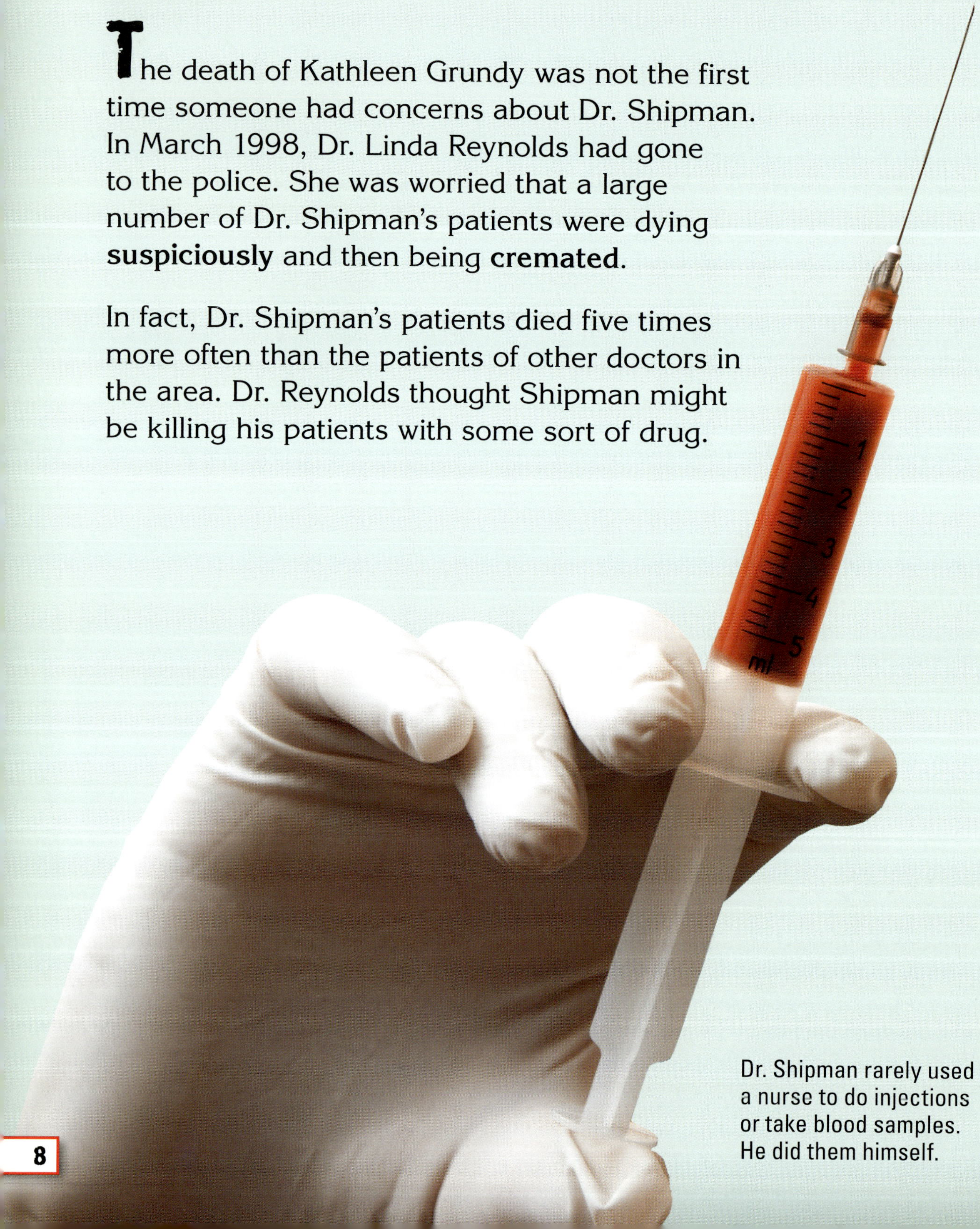

Dr. Shipman rarely used a nurse to do injections or take blood samples. He did them himself.

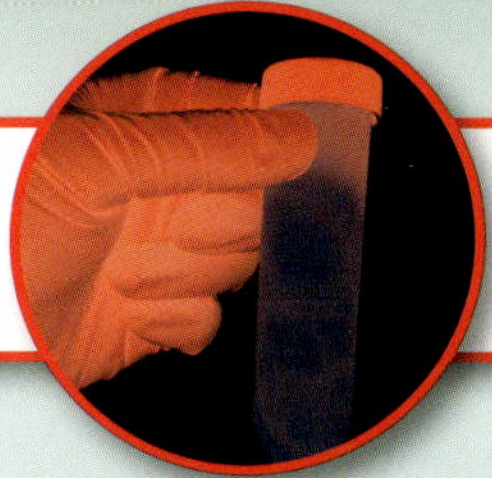

The police began an investigation of Dr. Shipman. However, they didn't do a very good job. They didn't get **toxicology** reports on two of Shipman's patients who had just died. The reports might have shown whether the patients had been poisoned or drugged.

Dr. Shipman (top right) with his coworkers in 1995

The police looked mainly at the death certificates, which seemed to be in order. After a month, they told Dr. Reynolds that Shipman was innocent. The police would soon learn how wrong they were.

FACT FILE

Missed Chances

- The police did not check Dr. Shipman's criminal record during their first investigation in March 1998.
- The police did not know that Shipman had broken the law by using his position as a doctor to steal painkilling drugs. He was **addicted** to them.
- Dr. Shipman was fined and forced to go into a drug **rehabilitation** center in 1975. However, he was allowed to continue practicing medicine.

Detective Inspector Dave Smith led the first investigation.

The Exhumation

When Angela Woodruff went to the police with her concerns, they decided to take another look at Dr. Shipman. In order to learn more about Mrs. Grundy's death, they needed to examine her body.

On the night of August 1, 1998, they **exhumed** her body from its **grave**. The date was exactly one month after she had been buried.

Kathleen Grundy's body was buried in Hyde Chapel Cemetery.

The police carried out the exhumation at night so it would not attract attention.

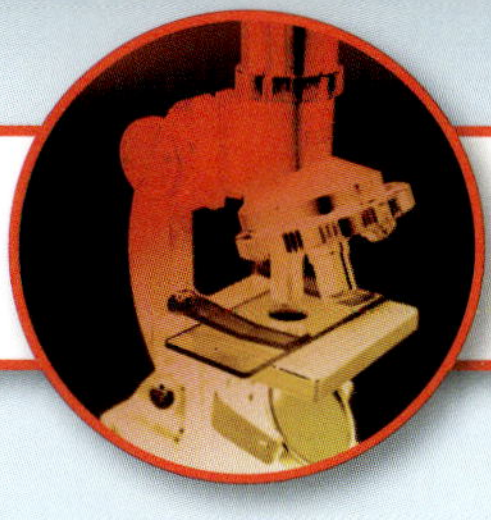

A **forensic pathologist** performed an **autopsy** on Mrs. Grundy's body. It showed that she didn't die of old age. She did not have a heart attack, as Dr. Shipman had also claimed. The forensic pathologist sent small samples of her muscle and liver to a lab. There they ran toxicology tests to see if she had been poisoned. The samples contained a drug called morphine—in an amount large enough to kill her.

A toxicology test is carried out on a sample of muscle tissue.

FACT FILE

Morphine

- Morphine is a painkiller used in hospitals.
- Police were surprised that Dr. Shipman would use morphine to poison a patient. A doctor would know that this type of drug can stay in the human body for years. It has even been found in Egyptian mummies that are thousands of years old!

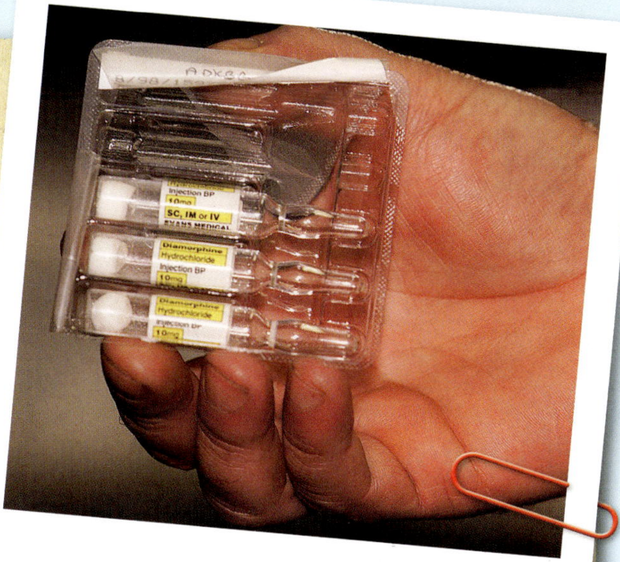

Morphine samples

Caught in a Lie

Police confronted Dr. Shipman with the news that Mrs. Grundy had died from a morphine **overdose**. Yet he didn't seem surprised. Dr. Shipman responded by saying Mrs. Grundy was a morphine **addict**. He had handwritten notes in her medical chart to back up his claim. However, Kathleen Grundy's hair had been tested for morphine use during the autopsy. These tests showed that Kathleen Grundy did not regularly take morphine—as an addict would.

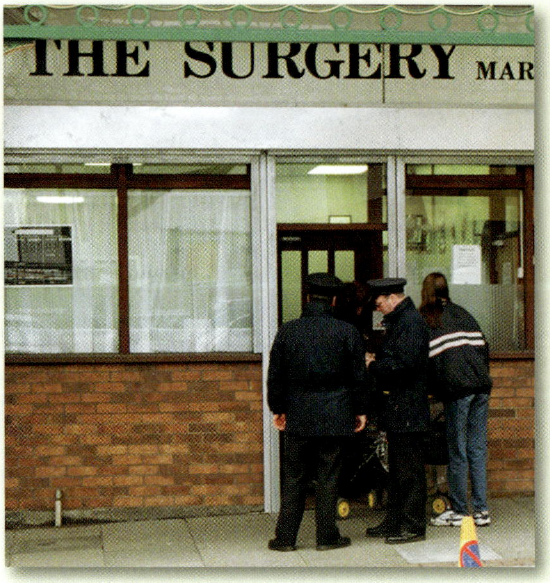

Security guards outside Dr. Shipman's office

In August 1998, police searched Dr. Shipman's home and office. They found large amounts of morphine. They took copies of his medical records and the office computer's **hard drive** as **evidence**.

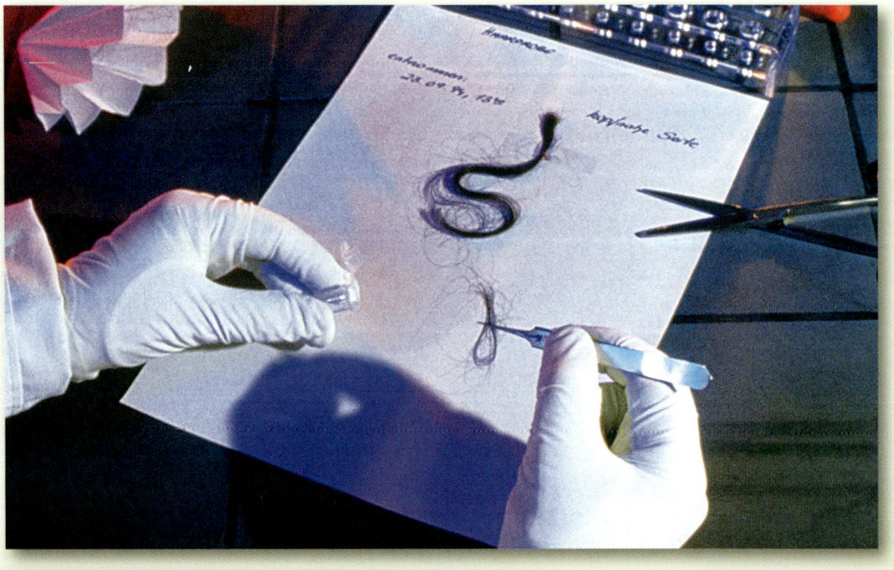

Experts examined Mrs. Grundy's hair for traces of morphine.

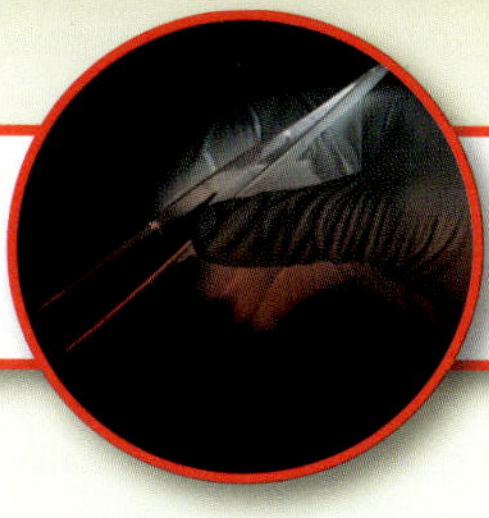

Police also found a typewriter. They determined it had been used to write Kathleen Grundy's new will. Dr. Shipman claimed Kathleen Grundy had borrowed it. However, when the police dusted the typewriter for fingerprints, they did not find any belonging to Mrs. Grundy.

The typewriter used to write Mrs. Grundy's will

FACT FILE

Credit Card Records

Harold Shipman had recorded fake medical appointments with Kathleen Gundy. The police could tell this by comparing his appointment book with his credit card bills.

- Every time a person uses a credit card, an electronic message is sent to the credit card company. The company makes a record of the date, time, and location of the card's use.
- Harold Shipman had recorded in his files an appointment with Kathleen Grundy in Hyde. However, his credit card records showed that he was actually on a shopping trip in York on that day.

Grave Evidence

On September 7, 1998, Dr. Shipman was **charged** with Mrs. Grundy's murder. The police suspected that she was not Dr. Shipman's only victim. They wanted to find out whether he had murdered others. So police had more of his patients' bodies exhumed.

Over four months, 11 female patients who died suspiciously were removed from their graves. Some of the bodies had been buried as long as six years. All were given toxicology tests.

A tent was placed over each grave to shield it from view.

The tests showed that eight of these patients had died from morphine overdoses. Yet none were morphine addicts. Their medical records showed that they had never been given the drug. Dr. Shipman must have secretly given it to them. The police now had evidence that Dr. Shipman was a **serial killer**.

Harold Shipman was suspected of killing a number of his patients.

FACT FILE

Burning the Evidence

Harold Shipman had tried to hide the cause of his patients' deaths by having his victims cremated.

- In Kathleen Grundy's fake will, Dr. Shipman requested that her body be cremated. Angela Woodruff did not know about the will until weeks after her mother's death. Luckily, she had been buried before the fake will turned up.
- If Mrs. Grundy's body had been cremated, police may never have found out how she really died.

After the autopsy, the victims' bodies were returned to their graves.

The Deadly Doctor

During their investigation, police began to learn more about how Dr. Shipman's patients died. The doctor was well known in Hyde for his willingness to treat people in their homes. His records showed that he was often the last person to see his patients alive.

Police learned that many of the victims were found lying down, as if asleep. The clothes they were wearing were neat and tidy. If the patients had suffered a stroke or a heart attack, as Dr. Shipman claimed on their death certificates, they would not have just lain down and drifted off. There would have been signs of a struggle. Their clothes might have been twisted or ripped.

Most of Harold Shipman's victims were women.

Since Dr. Shipman had visited his patients near the time when they died, he could determine the cause of death. He was also able to write out the death certificates. This way of working allowed him to kill patients without other doctors noticing.

Dr. Shipman worked on his own so other doctors would not know what he was doing.

FACT FILE

Call for Help

If someone else was home when Dr. Shipman killed a patient, he would often ask if he could use the phone to call an ambulance.

- The records of the Greater Manchester Ambulance Service showed, however, that Dr. Shipman did not actually call anyone.
- He pretended to call so no one would suspect the death was his fault.

Dr. Shipman failed to call an ambulance, even when he was with his patients as they died.

A Computer Error

Harold Shipman was clever. Yet he could not talk his way out of all of the evidence against him.

Dr. Shipman claimed that the errors police found in his patients' files were mistakes he had made because he had been rushing. His computer's hard drive, however, showed the true, terrible pattern.

Dr. Shipman's office

Dr. Shipman wanted to make it look like his patients had been ill before they died. So he changed the computer files of his victims within hours of murdering them. The hard drive made a record of when these changes were made. Computer experts were able to access these records, which helped prove Dr. Shipman's guilt.

A computer's hard drive

FACT FILE

Revealing Records

Maureen Ward was one of Dr. Shipman's victims.

- According to Shipman's computer records, he had noted that she had signs of a brain tumor for two months before she died.
- Shipman had also noted this "fact" on her death certificate.
- After looking at the computer's hard drive, computer experts saw that Shipman's notes had been added on the day that Mrs. Ward died.

Harold Shipman claimed Maureen Ward died of a brain tumor on February 18, 1998.

The Police Interviews

Dr. Shipman thought he could easily explain to the police why so many of his patients died. After all, he was a well-respected doctor in the community.

Shipman tried to use complicated medical language to confuse the police. He also told them, "People do die suddenly of old age. They just wear out."

Dr. Shipman (right) with police officers after his arrest

Dr. Shipman knew a lot about medicine. He did not know as much about computers, however.

On October 7, 1998, police spoke to Dr. Shipman about the computer records for three of his patients. He admitted that he had entered all of the notes in these patients' computer records. Police then showed him the proof from the hard drive that Shipman had made up the notes to support his cause of death.

Confronted with the evidence, Dr. Shipman fell to his knees, sobbing. He was charged with the murders of Joan Melia, Winifred Mellor, and Bianka Pomfret.

The computer evidence was the key to proving Shipman's guilt.

FACT FILE

Computers Don't Lie

Dr. Shipman claimed Winifred Mellor had died from a heart attack.

- A few hours after Winifred Mellor died, his computer's hard drive showed that Dr. Shipman added notes to her chart. He added entries to say she had been having heart trouble for years.
- Toxicology tests proved she actually died of a morphine overdose.

Winifred Mellor

Guilty

By February 1999, police had enough evidence to charge Dr. Shipman with the murder of 15 women. His trial began on October 5, 1999, and lasted four months. His wife and four children attended nearly every day. Throughout the trial, Dr. Shipman claimed he was innocent.

After the jury heard all of the evidence, they took six days to reach a **verdict**. On January 31, 2000, they found Dr. Shipman guilty of all 15 murders.

Manchester Evening News

SHIPMAN SPECIAL

BT NORTH WEST DAILY NEWSPAPER OF THE YEAR

Monday January 31 2000

www.manchesteronline.co.uk

30p

SHIPMAN TO SPEND REST OF LIFE IN JAIL

BY STEVE PANTER AND MICHAELA SITFORD

FAMILY GP Harold Shipman was tonight given 15 life sentences after being convicted of murdering 15 women patients for pleasure.

TURN TO PAGE 2

GUILTY!

Dr. Shipman was found guilty of murder.

Shipman received 15 life sentences and an additional four years for **forging** Mrs. Grundy's will. The judge in the case said, "None of your victims realized that yours was not a healing touch. None of them knew that in truth you had brought death, death which was disguised as the caring attention of a good doctor."

Harold Shipman was sent to Wakefield Prison.

FACT FILE

What Happened to Harold Shipman?

- After he was found guilty, Dr. Shipman was imprisoned in Frankland Prison, near Durham, England.
- He was then moved to Wakefield Prison, in West Yorkshire.
- He hanged himself in his cell on January 13, 2004.
- Dr. Shipman never admitted his guilt.

The Shipman Inquiry

A year after Dr. Shipman was sent to prison, an **inquiry** was set up by the British government. It looked into the deaths of 494 of his patients over a 24-year period from 1974 to 1998. The goal was to determine if Dr. Shipman had murdered other patients.

Between 2001 and 2005, the Shipman Inquiry took about 2,500 witness statements. It put together more than 270,000 pages of evidence.

The Shipman Inquiry looked into the deaths of Dr. Shipman's patients.

On July 19, 2002, the inquiry released a report. In addition to the 15 victims from the court case, the inquiry determined that Harold Shipman had killed 200 people and that there was a "real suspicion" about 45 more deaths.

Dame Janet Smith ran the Shipman Inquiry.

FACT FILE

Why Did He Kill?

- Dr. Shipman never told anyone why he killed his patients.
- South Manchester **coroner** John Pollard knew and worked with Shipman.
- He said Shipman "simply enjoyed viewing the process of dying and enjoyed the feeling of control over life and death."

Dr. Shipman never admitted that he killed anyone.

Case Closed

June 24, 1998

Kathleen Grundy is found dead at her home in Hyde, England. Dr. Shipman writes on her death certificate that she died of old age.

July 4, 1998

Mrs. Grundy's daughter, Angela Woodruff, receives a will that leaves everything to Dr. Harold Shipman. Thinking the will has been forged, she contacts the police.

August 1, 1998

Police exhume Kathleen Grundy's body. The autopsy shows that she had been killed by an overdose of the drug morphine.

August 7, 1998

Police search Dr. Shipman's house. They find large amounts of morphine.

August 14, 1998

Police search Dr. Shipman's office. They find the typewriter that Shipman used to write Mrs. Grundy's fake will. The police also take copies of Dr. Shipman's written records and the hard drive from his office computer.

September 7, 1998

Dr. Shipman is charged with the murder of Kathleen Grundy.

February 22, 1999

After the bodies of 14 more patients are exhumed, Dr. Shipman is charged with their murders.

October 5, 1999

Harold Shipman's trial begins.

January 31, 2000

Dr. Shipman is found guilty of murdering 15 of his patients. He is sentenced to life in prison.

July 19, 2002

The Shipman Inquiry reports that Harold Shipman murdered between 215 and 260 people from 1975 to 1998.

January 13, 2004

Harold Shipman hangs himself in his cell.

Crime Solving Up Close

Exhumations

Exhumations are carried out when the police need to examine a body that has already been buried. As Dr. Shipman was the only doctor to examine his patients after they died, police had to dig up the bodies to determine their cause of death.

- Exhumations normally take place at night so that they can be as private as possible.
- During an exhumation, a white tent is set up over the grave. This hides the process from onlookers.
- After the exhumation, a forensic pathologist performs an autopsy.
- The body is then reburied.

Four of Shipman's victims were exhumed from Hyde Cemetery.

Autopsy

When the police need to know how someone died, they will request that a forensic pathologist do an autopsy.

- The body is laid out on a table and thoroughly examined for injuries.
- The forensic pathologist makes a cut from behind the ear to the top of the leg to open up the body.
- The organs, including the stomach, lungs, and heart, are taken out and examined.
- Samples from the body are sent to a toxicology laboratory for testing. This is especially important if police think the person may have been poisoned. The lab checks to see if unusual drugs or poisons are in the body.
- The organs are then returned to the body which is sewn up. The body is then buried.

If an autopsy had been performed on any of Shipman's victims when they died, the doctor would have been caught much sooner.

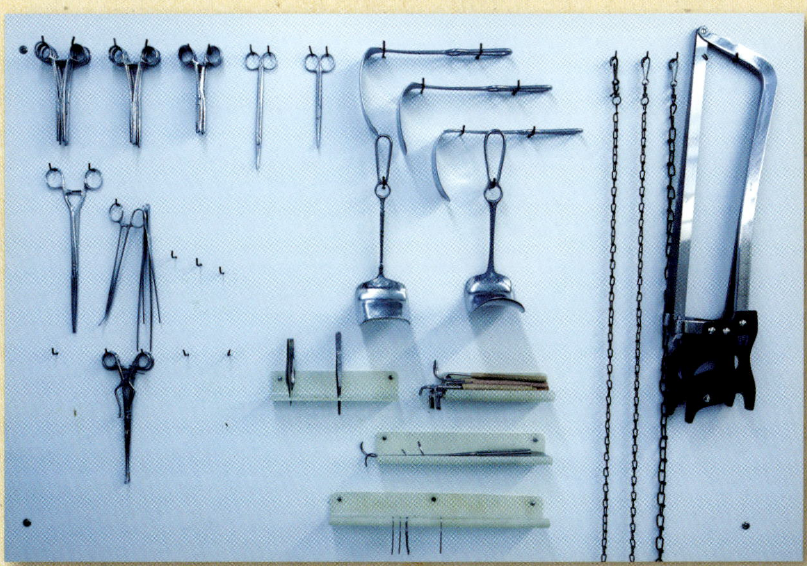

The tools used by forensic pathologists during an autopsy

Crime Solving Up Close

Toxicology

- Toxicology is the study of the harmful effects of drugs or poisons on people. It can show if these substances have caused someone to become ill or die.
- Police used toxicology in the Shipman case to find out how Harold Shipman's patients had died.
- Small amounts of hair, tissue, blood, or urine are tested with various chemicals to check for the presence of drugs or poisons.
- One kind of toxicology test examines hair. As hair grows, different chemicals are stored in it. By cutting a strand of hair into small pieces and testing each piece, forensic pathologists can measure how often a chemical or drug has been used by a person. Examining the hair of Shipman's victims showed that they were not regular morphine users.

Toxicologists use chemicals to test hair, tissue, and body fluids.

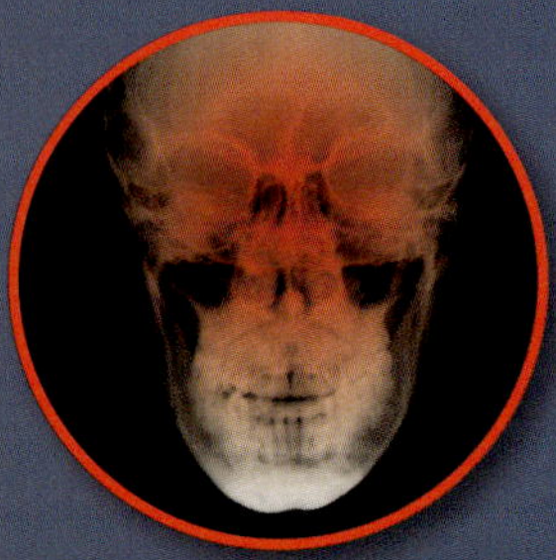

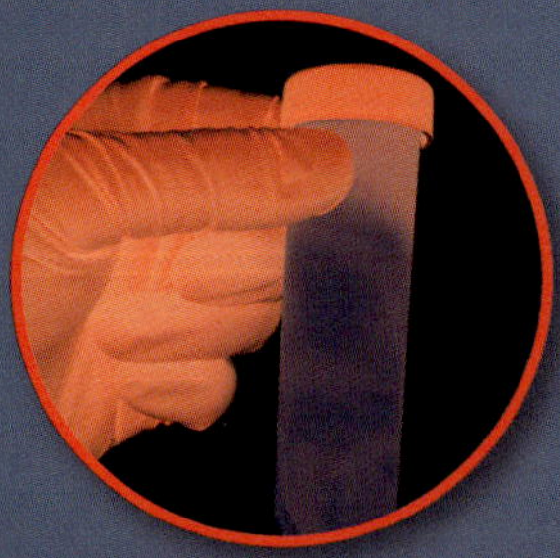

Glossary

addict (AD-ikt) a person who is unable to stop doing something

addicted (uh-DIK-tid) unable to stop doing or using something

autopsy (AW-top-see) an examination of a dead person that is used to find out the cause and time of death

charged (CHARJD) accused

coroner (KOR-uh-nur) a doctor who investigates suspicious deaths

cremated (KREE-mate-id) burned to ash

death certificate (DETH sur-TIF-uh-kit) a piece of paper that officially states a person's cause of death

evidence (EV-uh-duhnss) objects or information that can be used to prove whether something is true

exhumed (igz-OOMD) took a body out of its grave

forensic pathologist (fuh-REN-sik path-OL-uh-jist) a doctor who studies dead bodies to find out the cause of death

forging (FORJ-ing) making an illegal copy

grave (GRAYV) a hole dug in the ground where a dead person is buried

hard drive (HARD DRIVE) a device inside a computer where large amounts of data is stored

inquiry (in-KWYE-ree) an official investigation

investigate (in-VESS-tuh-*gate*) to find out about something

overdose (OH-vur-*dohss*) death or harm to a person that is caused by taking too much of a drug

rehabilitation (*ree*-huh-BIL-uh-*tay*-shun) restoring to good health

serial killer (SIHR-ee-uhl KIL-uhr) someone who murders more than one person

suspiciously (suh-SPISH-uhss-lee) a way of acting that causes question or doubt

toxicology (*toks*-uh-KOL-uh-jee) the study of the effect of poisonous substances on the body

verdict (VUR-dikt) a decision given to the court by a jury

will (WIL) written instructions explaining what should happen to a person's belongings when he or she dies

witnesses (WIT-niss-ez) people who tell what they saw

Index

Read More

Lane, Brian, and Laura Buller. *Crime & Detection.* New York: Dorling Kindersley (2005).

Libal, Angela. *Fingerprints, Bite Marks, Ear Prints: Human Signposts.* Broomall, PA: Mason Crest Publishers (2005).

Owen, David. *Police Lab: How Forensic Science Tracks Down and Convicts Criminals.* Canada: Firefly Books (2002).

Learn More Online

To learn more about crime solving and the Harold Shipman case, visit
www.bearportpublishing.com/CrimeSolvers

About the Author

Mikaela Sitford is a journalist and author of *Addicted to Murder: The True Story of Dr. Harold Shipman.* She is currently Media Relations Officer at the University of Manchester in England.